Help the
Green Turtles

by Grace Hansen

Abdo
Kids

LITTLE ACTIVISTS:
ENDANGERED SPECIES

Abdo Kids Jumbo is an Imprint of Abdo Kids
abdobooks.com

abdobooks.com

Published by Abdo Kids, a division of ABDO, P.O. Box 398166, Minneapolis, Minnesota 55439.
Copyright © 2019 by Abdo Consulting Group, Inc. International copyrights reserved in all countries.
No part of this book may be reproduced in any form without written permission from the publisher.
Abdo Kids Jumbo™ is a trademark and logo of Abdo Kids.

102018

012019

Photo Credits: Alamy, iStock, Minden Pictures, National Geographic Creative, Shutterstock

Production Contributors: Teddy Borth, Jennie Forsberg, Grace Hansen

Design Contributors: Dorothy Toth, Laura Mitchell

Library of Congress Control Number: 2018946052
Publisher's Cataloging-in-Publication Data

Names: Hansen, Grace, author.

Title: Help the green turtles / by Grace Hansen.

Description: Minneapolis, Minnesota : Abdo Kids, 2019 | Series: Little activists:
   endangered species | Includes glossary, index and online resources (page 24).

Identifiers: ISBN 9781532182006 (lib. bdg.) | ISBN 9781532182983 (ebook) |
   ISBN 9781532183478 (Read-to-me ebook)

Subjects: LCSH: Green turtle--Juvenile literature. | Wildlife recovery--Juvenile
   literature. | Endangered species--Juvenile literature. | Black sea turtle--Juvenile
   literature.

Classification: DDC 333.954--dc23

Table of Contents

Green Turtles

Green turtles are sea turtles.
They mainly live near coasts
in warm ocean waters.

Green turtles can grow to be 700 pounds (318 kg). And unlike most sea turtles, they only eat plants.

Status

Green turtles are **endangered** around the world. Especially those that live in the Mediterranean Sea.

8

Threats

Green turtles face many threats.

Many are captured for their

meat and shells. Sometimes,

their eggs are stolen.

10

Pollution is another threat. Green turtles may eat plastic accidentally. Recycling and reducing the use of plastic is important.

Green turtles can get captured in fishing nets. Special nets have been made to keep sea turtles from getting caught.

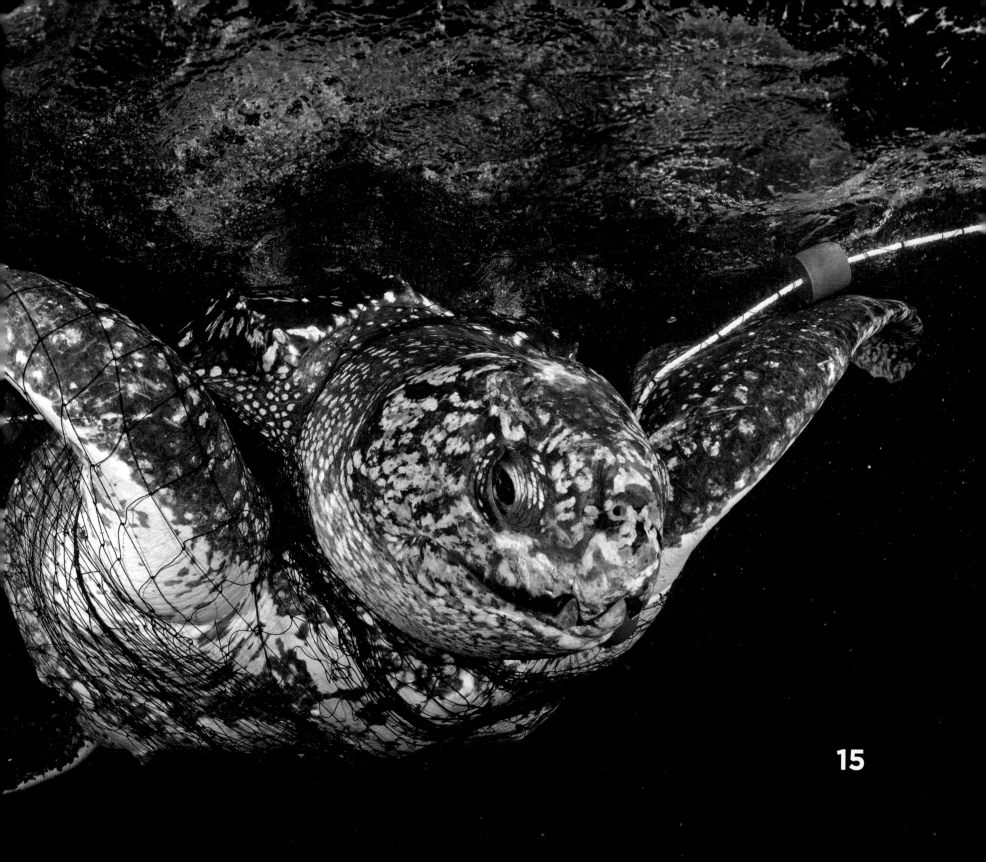

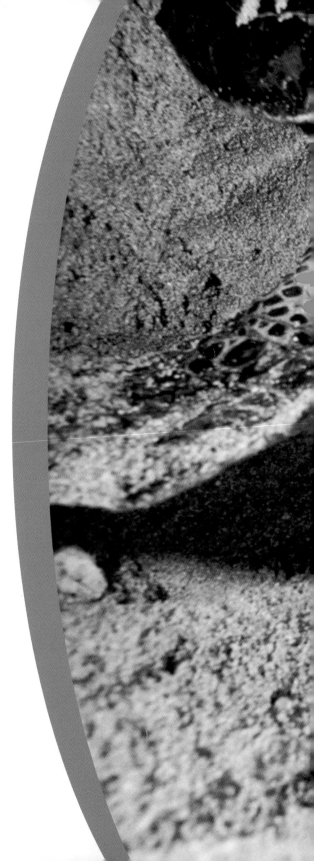

Green turtles can live for more than 80 years. They cannot lay eggs until they are around 30 years old. Protecting them for years to come is necessary for population growth.

Why They Matter

Green sea turtles eat **seagrass**.

This keeps seagrass healthy.

Many other ocean animals

depend on seagrass for shelter.

Happily, green sea turtle populations are on the rise. More people are seeing them nest each year. Their rising numbers show that other ocean habitats are healthy too!

Green Turtles Overview

- Status: **Endangered**

- Population: 80,000–100,000 nesting females

- Habitat: Tropical and subtropical ocean waters

- Greatest Threats: Illegal hunting, **pollution**, fish nets, and warming seas

Glossary

endangered – in danger of becoming extinct.

pollution – poisons, wastes, or other materials that can pollute.

seagrass – flowering plants that grow in marine, salty environments. They give marine animals shelter, make oxygen, protect coasts from erosion, and store carbon dioxide.

Index

**Abdo Kids
ONLINE**
FREE! ONLINE MULTIMEDIA RESOURCES

Visit **abdokids.com** and use this code to access crafts, games, videos, and more!

Abdo Kids Code:
LHK2006